Irish Vegetarian Cookery

Also by Patrick Cotter

Poetry
The Misogynist's Blue Nightmare
A Socialist's Dozen
Love Poems (forthcoming)

As editor
The Cloverdale Anthology Of New Irish Poetry Volumes 1 & 2

Irish Vegetarian Cookery

Edited
By
Patrick Cotter

Three
Spires
Press

Published in Ireland by
Three Spires Press
Killeen,
Blackrock Village,
Cork City.

First published in 1993

Typeset, by Three Spires Press, in Insignia, Garamond and Hobo on PageMaker 4 for Windows output to a Hewlett-Packard Laserjet 4
Printed by Lee Press, Cork

This book is dedicated to my mother and father, Mary & Tom and I.M. Colin Long 1969-1993

Please note!

If you are gentle with this book it will last a long time. If you double-back the covers, or jerk them back as you open the book, you are increasing the risk of the book's spine breaking.

Cover design by Patrick Cotter incorporating a stained glass window by James Scanlon *Gleann Na Luachra* Triskel Arts Centre

Contents

Glossary

There are just a handful of terms with which some readers might be unfamiliar- I list them hereunder:

Garam Masala is an blend of spices popular in Indian cookery available from any large supermarket or more cheaply from a good wholefood shop.

Pine kernals, also known as pine nuts, are available from any good wholefood store.

Tahini is an oil derived from sesame seeds and can be got from a good wholefood store.

Fyllo pastry is a special thin pastry which can be bought in sheets from supermarkets.

Preface

I was seventeen before I handled my first sweet pepper, let alone ate one. Many vegetables and ingredients that seemed highly exotic (and expensive!) in Ireland a decade ago are now quite commonplace in our small and large towns. Their availability and high profile today has led to a revolution in Irish kitchens. No longer are most people satisfied with the meat and two veg. combos (usually over-boiled to tastless mush) which our fathers demanded and received.

As little as twenty years ago in Ireland vegetarians were considered as being in the same league as Martians. My first encounter with vegetarians happened when I was a boy: a family of Punjabis moved to our street. Both our families became very good friends and it was inevitable that I should be introduced to the exotic mysteries of Indian cuisine. I was amazed with what they were able to do with potatoes, but something in my background made me feel sorry for them because their religion forbid them to eat meat. As a typical Irishman I believed a dinner wasn't a dinner unless there was a slab of burnt flesh on my plate. Yet this typical Irish attitude is, historically, only a recent phenomenon. For most of our history most of our people could not afford meat and survived quite ably on vegetables and dairy products. Ireland's population swelled to 8 million on a mainly vegetarian diet. With all our recent investment in meat production and consumption we have not been able to sustain that population at home.

Irish cuisine is particularly reliant on dairy products and breads. These ingredients are two very important nutrition blocks in a vegetarian's diet: Irish cuisine has much to offer international vegetarian cuisine (For more details on nutrition and eating the right combinations of food I recommend Rose Eliot's *The Supreme Vegetarian Cookbook* as an esential guide). Irish Vegetarian Cookery has been primarily an act of collation rather than authorship. I have altered most of the traditional recipes slightly - as every cook should, to adjust to their own particular tastes and kitchen equipment. To the creative cook, recipes should always be looked upon only as guidelines. These traditional recipes form the first part of the book whose purpose is twofold: first to acquaint people with the repertoire of Irish vegetarian cuisine and secondly to form a simple introduction to vegetarian cooking, as most of the ingredients used are proverbial in an Irish context and the methods are uncomplicated. I have also included some of my own simple and undemanding (but tasty) inventions.

For the more adventurous I have invited gourmet restaurants from around the country to submit samples of vegetarian starters, maincourses and desserts from their menus. I would have liked to have included a restaurant from Northern Ireland but none responded to my request. Cork as befitting the gourmet capital of the country provides the most contributions. Like a national language, a national cuisine is never static: just as a language borrows words and phrases from another language to make them its own, so too do national cuisines appropriate ingredients and cooking methods. The recipes from professional cooks in *part two* serve to illustrate the revolutionary cutting-edge of Irish cuisine today.

There are three main reasons why different people choose to eat vegetarian: 1) because its healthlier 2) because they believe its more moral 3) because its tastier. Like myself you can still be an occasional carnivore and still like vegetarian food for reason 3.

If I had one wish in connection with this book it would be to rescue from culinary drudgery all those teenage fans of Morrissey I hear about and occasionally meet; surviving on little more than chips, peas and curry sauce, whilst lecturing us, in their youthful enthusiasm, that meat is murder.

Pat Cotter

Home Recipes

Cream Of Mushroom Soup

Ingredients

40g (1½oz) butter
1 large onion finely chopped
2 stalks of celery finely chopped
350 g (12oz) of finely chopped mushrooms
25 g (1oz) plain flour
25 g (1oz) butter
600 ml(1 pint) vegetable stock
150 ml(5 fl oz) cream
1 teaspoon of dried mixed herbs
paprika
salt & pepper
4 perfectly-shaped button mushrooms sliced lengthways and fried until brown

Method

1 Melt the butter in a saucepan. Fry onion and celery until soft.

2 Add finely chopped mushrooms, herbs, salt & pepper. Cook gently
until mushroom juice evaporates.

3 Stir in flour and cook for 1-2 minutes. Add stock and bring to the boil, stirring occasionally.

4 Add cream, whisk and reheat without boiling.

5 garnish each bowl with pre-fried mushroom slices and sprinkles of paprika.

Nettle Soup

Ingredients

25 g (1oz) butter
50 g (2oz) oatmeal
600 ml (1 pint) of washed, finely-chopped, young, spring, stinging-nettle tops
1 large chopped onion
600 ml (1 pint) milk
300 ml (½ pint) vegetable stock
salt & pepper
chopped fresh parsley
300 ml (½ pint) cream

Method

1 Melt the butter and fry the oatmeal until brown

2 Pour in the stock and milk. Bring to the boil.

3 Add the nettles and onion, salt and pepper. Simmer for 45 minutes

4 Add parsley and cream

5 Liquidise if desired

6 Reheat before serving

Potato Soup

Ingredients

900 g (2 lb.) potatoes peeled and diced.
2 leeks peeled and chopped or 2 onions if preferred
25 g (1oz) butter
450 ml (¾ pint) milk
450 ml (¾ pint) vegetable stock
salt & pepper
1 clove of garlic peeled and crushed (optional)
90 ml (4 tablespoons) Cream

Method

1 Melt the butter in a saucepan. Add the garlic and vegetables and cook gently until soft.

2 Pour in the milk and stock. Add salt & pepper to taste.

3 Bring to the boil and simmer gently for 1 hour.

4 Whisk in cream and reheat before serving.

Pea Soup

Ingredients

25 g (1 oz butter)
1 onion chopped
1 carrot diced
1 clove garlic crushed
2 celery sticks chopped
250 g (8oz) dried marrow fat peas, soaked overnight
750 ml water
750 ml vegetable stock
1 teaspoon dried mixed herbs
Salt & pepper
90 ml (4 tablespoons) cream

Method

1 Melt butter in saucepan. Add the onion and carrot and cook gently until onion is softened.

2 Add the garlic and celery and cook for 5 minutes.

3 Drain the peas and add to the saucepan along with the water, stock, herbs and salt & pepper to taste. Cover and boil for ten minutes, then simmer for 2 to 3 hours, until the peas are soft.

4 Allow to cool slightly, then liquidise with cream to a smooth paste. Add more cream or water if too thick.

5 Reheat the soup before serving. Garnish with mint.

Brotchen Roy

Ingredients

3 Leeks
25g (1oz) butter
75g (3oz) flake oatmeal
600ml (1 pint) vegetable stock
300ml (½ pint) milk
Salt and pepper to taste
A pinch of mace
Chopped parley
2 tablespoons of cream

Method

1 Wash the leeks thoroughly and chop into chunks.

2 Melt the butter gently in a saucepan not allowing it to brown.

3 Add the oatmeal and fry it in the butter, stirring until golden brown.

4 Still stirring, pour on the stock and milk.

5 Add the chopped leeks, salt, pepper and mace.

6 Bring to the boil, and then simmer for about 30 minutes until the broth is thick.

7 Put the soup through a sieve or liquidise in a blender.

8 Reheat gently.

9 Stir in the cream and parsley not allowing the soup to boil again before serving with Irish Soda Bread.

Champ

Ingredients

450g (1 lb) potatoes
8 spring onions or 1 onion
90ml milk
50g (2oz) butter
Salt and pepper

Method

1 Peel and slice the potatoes and simmer in a saucepan of salted water until tender.

2 Drain, and mash well and keep hot.

3 Chop the spring onions using the green as well as the white parts or peel and chop the onion.

4 Cook the chopped onions in the milk until soft.

5 Beat the hot milk, onions and pepper into the potatoes.

6 The mixture should be soft and fluffy but not sloppy.

7 Pile into a warm serving dish.

8 Make a hole in the centre and put in the butter.

9 For an interesting variation cook two crushed cloves of garlic with the onions in step 3

Colcannon

Ingredients

450g (1lb) potatoes
Salt and pepper
450g (1lb) white cabbage
100 ml milk
100 ml cream
1 onion
100g (4oz) butter
Chopped parsley

Method

1 Peel , boil and mash the potatoes.

2 Allow to cool a little, then add cream

3 Cook the cabbage in boiling salted water until tender.

4 Drain well, and chop.

5 Peel and chop the onion finely

6 Add the onions to the milk.

7 Bring to the boil and simmer until tender.

8 Add the cooked cabbage, onions and milk to the potatoes. Season with pepper, and more salt if required.

9 Keep stirring over the heat, without letting the Colcannon brown.

10 Mix in the butter until melted

Beetroot and Potato

Ingredients

75g (3oz) butter
3 Medium-sized cooked beets, peeled and sliced.
2 Small onions, sliced
50g (2oz) flour
300ml (½ pint) milk mixed with 50ml cream
Salt and pepper
1 Teaspoon sugar
1 Tablespoon vinegar
700g (1½lb) mashed potato, kept hot

Method

1 Heat a little of the butter and fry onions in it until soft, but do not let them brown.

2 Heat the rest of the butter, stir in the flour and cook for about 1 minute.

3 Then add the milk and cream stirring all the time. Season well with salt & pepper

4 Stir in the sugar and the vinegar and cook for about 1 minute, then add the beet slices.

5 Make a circle of the hot mashed potatoes, place the beetroot and sauce in the middle.

Baked Onions

Ingredients

4 large onions, unpeeled
Salt and pepper
Some butter

Method

1 Place the onions in an oven proof dish . Pour in enough water to the depth of one third of the onions height

2 Bake in a moderate oven for about 1½ hours, or until the onions are soft .

3 Sprinkle with salt and pepper.

4 Just before serving top each onion with a knob of butter.

Oven: 160 °C

Creamed Cabbage

Ingredients

1kg (2¼lb) white cabbage
50g (2oz) butter
25g (1oz) flour
Pinch of grated nutmeg
300ml milk
300ml cream
Salt and pepper

Method

1 Trim the cabbage, removing the stalk, cut into eighths and blanch for 5 minutes in boiling salted water.

2 Drain well, then cut into strips.

3 Heat the butter, stir in the flour and cook for 1 minute, then gradually add the milk and cream, then the nutmeg, stirring well to avoid lumps.

4 Add the cabbage and bring back to the boil.

5 Cover and cook gently for 15 minutes, stirring from time to time.

6 Serve the cabbage, while still crunchy

Creamed Swedes

Ingredients

450g (1lb) swedes
Salt and pepper
25g (1 oz) butter
2 Tablespoons cream
A pinch of paprika

Method

1 Peel and cut up the Swedes.

2 Put in a saucepan of cold, salted water.

3 Bring to the boil and simmer until tender.

4 Drain and mash.

5 Mix in the butter.

6 Season well with pepper.

7 Add the paprika, and stir in the cream.

8 Serve hot.

Fried Parsnips

Ingredients

4 Parsnips
100g (4oz) butter
Salt and pepper

Method

1 Wash and clean the parsnips, cut across in short pieces, about 2.5cm (1 inch).

2 Add seasoning to water and boil for about half an hour.

3 Drain and dry.

4 Heat the butter in a pan and fry parsnips in it.

5 Brown under grill.

Parsnips Cakes

Ingredients

450g (1lb) parsnips
75g (30z) flour
Pinch garam masala (see glossary)
50g (2oz) melted butter
Salt and pepper
1 large egg beaten
4 slices of stale bread reduced to crumbs
Butter for frying

Method

1 Peel and slice the parsnips, then boil in salted water until tender.

2 Drain and mash them well.

3 Add the flour, garam masala, melted butter, salt and pepper and form into flat cakes.

4 Dip into the beaten egg, then into breadcrumbs and fry in hot butter until brown on both sides.

Boxty Cakes

Ingredients

450g (1½lb) cooked mashed potatoes
450g (1½lb) raw potatoes, peeled and grated
Some milk
A pinch of salt.
450g (1½lb) Flour
Butter for serving

Method

1 Mix the raw and cooked potatoes together, and season to taste with a pinch of salt.

2 Work in enough flour and milk to give a pliable dough.

3 Knead well and roll out.

4 Shape into 4 rounds.

7 Place on a greased tray and bake in a hot oven for 30-45 minutes at 160°C

8 Butter and serve hot.

Spicy Boxty Cakes

Ingredients

225g (9oz) cooked, mashed potatoes
225g (9oz) cooked , mashed carrots
400g (1 lb.) raw potatoes, peeled and grated
400g (1 lb.) flour
150g (6oz) precooked mushy peas
some milk
½ teaspoon turmeric
2 teaspoons of garam masala (see glossary)
a pinch of salt

Method

1 Mix together the cooked and raw vegetables.

2 Sieve the flour, salt and spices into vegetable mixture

3 Mix to form dough, adding milk if necessary

Repeat steps 4-8 as for ordinary Boxties

Potato And Thyme Cakes

Ingredients

500g (1lb) potatoes
25g (1oz) butter
100g (4oz) plain flour
salt
2 tablespoons of fresh thyme or 2 teaspoons of dried thyme
for frying 75g (3oz) butter

Method

1 Scrub potatoes and boil for 20-30 minutes

2 Drain and allow to cool for a moment

3 Peel and mash

4 Add butter, salt and thyme

5 Mix with flour and form a dough

6 On a floured surface, roll out dough to a thickness of 1 cm and cut into 5 cm squares

7 Heat butter for frying in pan and fry cakes until crispy and golden on both sides

Lyonaise Potatoes

Ingredients

500g (1lb) potatoes
2 large onions, thinly sliced
250 ml cream
3 cloves of garlic crushed
salt and pepper
parsley

Method

1 Peel and wash potatoes, cut into slices

2 Place the potatoes and onion in alternate layers into an oven proof dish, sprinkling each layer with salt and pepper.

3 Sprinkle top layer with parsley and garlic

4 Pour over the cream

5 Place in a pre-heated oven at 200°C and leave for 45-60 minutes or until tender

Potato and Onion Mash

Ingredients

1kg (2lb) potatoes
1 large onion finely chopped
2 tablespoons of butter
1 teaspoon honey
a drop of milk
1 teaspoon of thyme
salt and pepper

Method

1 Peel and wash potatoes

2 Boil for 25-30 minutes

3 Melt 1 tablespoon of butter in a pan and fry onions, add honey and continue frying until onions are golden brown.

4 Drain potatoes and mash, add butter and milk

5 Season with salt, pepper and thyme

6 Mix in onions

Potato and Carrot Omellete

Ingredients

750g (1.5lb) potatoes
2 carrots diced
2 onions chopped
2 cloves garlic crushed
6 eggs
salt and pepper
mixed herbs
4 oz butter for frying

Method

1 Wash potatoes and boil for 25-30 minutes

2 Drain and allow to cool

3 Heat butter and fry carrots for three minutes

4 Add onion and garlic and fry for a further three minutes until golden, then set aside

5 Beat eggs in a large basin

6 Peel and slice potatoes

7 Mix everything in with the eggs

8 Reheat frying pan add mixture and cook until the egg congeals totally

9 Slip the pan under a pre-heated grill and leave until topside of omelette is golden.

Potato And Mushroom Pie

Ingredients

1kg (2lb) potatoes
500g (1lb) mushrooms, sliced in half.
75g (3oz) butter
300ml cream
4 egg yolks
1 onion chopped
salt and pepper
2 tablespoons Parmesan cheese

Method

1 Wash and peel potatoes, cut into cubes and cook for 25-30 minutes

2 Drain and mash

3 Melt 25g (1oz) butter and fry onion and mushrooms for about 5 minutes

4 Add seasoning and remove from heat

5 Stir in 50ml of cream

6 Mix potatoes with egg yolks, remaining butter and cream, season with salt and pepper

7 Preheat oven to 200°C

8 Spoon half of potato mixture into an oven proof pie dish and top with mushroom mixture, cover with remaining potatoes, cover with grated cheese and bake for 20 minutes

Vegetarian Shepherd's Pie

Ingredients

225g (8oz) yellow or green split peas
50g (2oz) butter
3 large onions diced
1 clove garlic crushed
1 teaspoon dried mixed herbs
1 can of tomatoes
2 tablespoons of Soya sauce
1 teaspoon thyme
700g (1.5lb) potatoes cooked and mashed
2 large carrots cooked and sliced

Method

1 Put the peas into a saucepan of water and boil gently for 45 minutes

2 Preheat the oven to 200°C.

3 Gently fry two of the onions in the butter in a large saucepan for 10 minutes.

4 Add the garlic, mixed herbs, tomatoes, Soya sauce, peas, carrots and salt and pepper to taste. Put aside

5 Mix the remaining onion and thyme with the potatoes, season with salt and pepper

6 Spoon the pea mixture into greased, shallow, oven-dish. Spread the potatoes over the top, flatten with a wooden spoon, then with a fork draw ridges across the surface.

7 Bake the pie for 45 minutes or until the potatoes are golden.

Potato and Tomato Bake

Ingredients

4 garlic cloves, peeled
1 teaspoon dried mixed herbs
300 ml water
8 potatoes thickly sliced
4 large tomatoes, skinned, seeded and sliced
salt and pepper

Method

1 Put the garlic, mixed herbs and water in a pan and simmer for 20-30 minutes.

2 Leave to cool

3 Crush the garlic with a pestle or the back of a fork until it forms a smooth mixture with the water and herbs.

4 Spoon half the mixture into a small oven-dish.

5 Layer the potatoes and tomatoes alternately on top and season well with salt and pepper.

6 Spoon over the remaining garlic mixture

7 Cover and cook in preheated, moderate oven 180°C for 1 hour or until the potatoes are tender.

Cotter's Buttermilk Stew

Ingredients

2 tablespoons oil
2 carrots diced finely
1 potato diced finely
1 onion finely chopped
225g (½ lb.) button mushrooms sliced
1 red pepper diced
1 green pepper diced
2 cloves garlic crushed
1 tin sweet corn drained
600ml (1 pint) buttermilk
200ml cream
1 vegetable stock cube
1 teaspoon mixed herbs
1 dash soy sauce

Method

1 Fry gently, carrots, potato and onion for three minutes without browning.

2 Add garlic, peppers and stock cube. Cook for 1 minute.

3 Pour in buttermilk with mixed herbs. Bring to boil. Allow to simmer for 20 minutes.

4 Add cream, sweet corn, Soya sauce and salt and pepper. Return to boil before serving with pasta shells or swirls.

Cotter's Bread Stuffing

Ingredients

4 slices of bread (brown or white or both)
1 onion
½ dessert apple
teaspoon mixed herbs
2 tablespoons white wine
2 cloves garlic
Salt and pepper

Method

1 Reduce bread to crumbs

2 Chop onion and apple finely

3 Crush garlic

4 Mix everything in a bowl

or alternatively

Put all the ingredients into a food processor and mix to a smooth paste.

Use to stuff sweet peppers and bake in a moderate oven 160°C for 45 minutes.

Buttermilk

Ingredients

15g (½ oz) sugar
15g (½ oz) yeast
300ml (½pint) warmed water
300ml (½ pint) milk

Method

1 Cream the sugar with the yeast.

2 Pour the milk into the warmed water.

3 Gradually stir in the sugar and yeast.

4 Cover and leave at room temperature for a day.

5 The liquid should smell slightly sour and taste slightly sour

6 Strain and the buttermilk is ready to use, or refrigerate

Barnbrack

Ingredients

300ml (½ pint) of black tea
350g (12 oz) brown sugar
225g (8 oz) raisins
225g (8 oz) sultanas
50g (2 oz) butter or margarine
1 large egg, beaten
50g (2 oz) cherries, chopped
50g (2 oz) candied peel
25g (1 oz) almonds chopped
275g (10 oz) flour
1 heaped teaspoon baking powder

Method

1 Dissolve the sugar in the tea.

2 Add the raisins and sultanas and leave to soak overnight.

3 Melt the butter and mix in with the beaten egg, cherries, candied peel and almonds.

4 Sieve the flour and baking powder and add to the egg and fruit mixture, mixing thoroughly.

5 Grease an 20cm (8 inch) cake tin and turn in the mixture.

6 A ring or coin can be added to mixture at this stage, once it has been wrapped in grease-proof paper.

7 Bake in a moderate oven 180° C for 1½ hours.

Brown Scones

Ingredients

750g (7oz) plain flour
750g (7oz) wholemeal flour
A pinch of salt
2 teaspoons baking powder
50g (2oz) sugar
100 g (4oz) butter
1 egg, beaten
1 cup of milk

Method

1 Mix plain flour and whole wheat flour.

2 Add salt, baking powder and sugar.

3 Rub in the butter with your fingers

4 Add beaten egg to milk, and gradually mix in enough milk to make a soft dough.

5 Knead lightly and turn onto a floured surface.

6 Cut into rounds 2.5 cm thick and place on a greased baking tray and bake at 220°C for 20 minutes approx.

Soda Bread

Ingredients

450g (1 lb.) flour
1 teaspoon bicarbonate of soda
1 tablespoon salt
300ml (½ pint) buttermilk or soured milk
1 egg beaten

Method

1 Sieve the dry ingredients together in a large mixing bowl.

2 Make a well in the centre and add the buttermilk and egg.

3 Knead until a smooth, soft dough forms.

4 Shape the dough into a flat cake and place on a greased sheet

5 Cut a deep cross into the dough so the bread can rise without splitting its crust.

6 Bake in a hot oven for about 35 minutes or until browned and risen.

7 Remove from the oven. If the bread is cooked it will sound hollow when tapped on the bottom.

Oven: 220°C

Brown Wholemeal Bread

Ingredients

350g (12 oz) wholemeal flour
350g (12 oz) plain flour
1 teaspoon salt
2 teaspoons baking powder
2 tablespoons bran
600ml (1 pint) buttermilk

Method

1 Mix all the dry ingredients in a large bowl.

2 Stir in the buttermilk.

3 Grease a 20cm (8 inch) cake tin, spoon in the mixture and cover with tinfoil.

10 Bake in an oven for 1 hour.

Oven: 220° C

Porter Cake

Ingredients

450g (1 lb.) flour
1 teaspoon of baking powder
A pinch of salt
1 teaspoon of mixed spice
225g (8oz) butter
225g (8 oz) brown sugar
1 teaspoon nutmeg
450g (1 lb.) mixed dried fruit
Grated rind of 1 lemon
3 eggs, beaten
300ml stout (Beamish or Murphys if possible)

Method

1 Sieve the flour with the salt into a mixing bowl.

2 Mix the baking powder, sugar and spice.

3 Rub in the butter.

4 Add the dried fruit, mixing thoroughly.

5 Mix the stout with the beaten eggs and blend into the cake mixture.

6 Grease and line a 20cm (8 inch) cake tin.

7 Pour in the mixture and bake in a moderately hot oven (160°) for an hour, then lower heat to 150° and bake for a further 2 hours

8 Allow to cool in the tin. This cakes flavour improves if left wrapped in foil for at least a week before eating.

Kinsale Bread

Ingredients

15g (½oz) yeast
400 ml warm water
2 tablespoons sugar
600g (1½lb) whole wheat flour
½ teaspoon salt
50 ml molasses
100 ml honey

Method

1 Preheat oven to 225°C

2 Dissolve yeast in 100 ml warm water and one tablespoon sugar. Set aside.

3 Take half of the flour and make a batter with the yeast mixture and remaining warm water.

4 Cover the bowl with a damp cloth and let stand for 15 minutes.

5 Add the rest of the flour, salt, molasses, sugar and honey. Beat with a wooden spoon until batter is stiff.

6 Knead on a floured surface for 10 minutes.

7 Place dough in pan, cover and place in a warm place for 1 hour or until dough doubles in size.

8 Bake for 45 minutes, turning the pan in the opposite direction halfway through the cooking time.
9 Remove from oven and place on a wire rack. Let bread stand for 20 minutes, remove from tin and cool thoroughly before serving.

Potato and Apple Pie

Ingredients

450g (1 lb.) mashed potatoes
50g (2 oz) butter
100g (4 oz) flour
A pinch of salt
½ teaspoon baking powder
3-4 apples
2 tablespoons sugar
25g (1 oz) butter
½ teaspoon cinnamon

Method

1 Mix the butter into the freshly mashed potatoes.

2 Sift the flour with the salt, cinnamon and baking powder.

3 Add the flour to the mashed potatoes and work to a dough.

4 Divide the dough and roll out on a floured surface into 2 rounds, one larger than the other. Place the larger one on a greased baking tray.

5 Peel, core and slice the apples.

6 Cover the pastry circle with the raw apple slices.

7 Dampen the edges and put the other pastry round on top, pressing together to seal the edges.

8 Bake in a moderately hot oven (190°) for 30-40 minutes or until golden brown.

9 Remove from the oven and carefully remove the upper crust.

10 Sprinkle the apples with sugar and cinnamon and dot with butter.

11 Replace the top and return to the oven for a few moments to allow the butter to melt.

12 Serve whilst hot.

Apple and Elderberry Pie

Ingredients

350g (12 oz) flour
A pinch of salt
350g (12 oz) butter
Some milk
4 large cooking apples
2 bunches of elderberries
75g (3 oz) sugar
Castor sugar for dusting
1 tablespoon honey

Method

1 Sieve the flour with the salt into a mixing bowl.

2 Rub the butter into the flour until it resembles fine breadcrumbs.

3 Add enough milk to form a stiff dough.

4 Leave the dough to stand at room temperature for about an hour.

5 Roll out half the pastry onto a floured surface.

6 Cut out a circle large enough to cover a 25cm (10 inch) plate.

7 Grease the plate with butter and line with the pastry.

8 Peel, core and finely slice the apples.

9 Wash elderberries and destalk.

10 Sprinkle the elderberries over the apples and pour 1 tablespoon of water unto fruit, cover also with sugar and honey.

11 Roll out the remaining pastry and use to cover the pie.

12 Dampen the edges with water and press well together.

13 Sprinkle with caster sugar.

14 Bake in a moderately hot 200°C for about 45 minutes or until the pastry is golden brown.

Christmas Plum Pudding

Ingredients

225g (8 oz) flour
A pinch of salt
1 teaspoon baking powder
2 teaspoons mixed spice
225g (8 oz) fresh breadcrumbs
225g (8 oz) butter
175g (6 oz) brown sugar
575g (14 oz) mixed dried fruit
50g (2 oz) glacé cherries,
50g (2 oz) candied peel
50g (2 oz) ground almonds,
2 eggs, beaten
2 tablespoons honey
150 ml whiskey
A drop of milk

Method

1 Sift together the flour, salt, baking powder and spice.

2 Add the breadcrumbs, butter and sugar, mixing everything well together.

3 Add the mixed fruit, cherries, candied peel and almonds.

4 Add the beaten eggs, honey, whiskey and enough milk to make a soft pudding mixture.

5 Mix everything thoroughly.

6 Grease a pudding basin and fill with the mixture allowing space at the top of the basin for the pudding to rise.

7 Cover the basin with 2 sheets of grease proof paper, securely tied.

8 Steam in a pan of boiling water for about 5 hours. Do not allow the pan to boil dry. Top up the water in the pan regularly.

9 Serve flaming with more whiskey.

Home Made Custard Sauce

Ingredients

450ml (¾ pint) milk
150ml (¼ pint) cream
1 egg
1 egg yolk
1 teaspoon vanilla flavouring
25g (1 oz) sugar or to taste.

Method

1 Put a saucepan of cold water on the stove to boil.

2 Beat the eggs, sugar and vanilla flavouring together until fluffy.

3 Heat the milk and gradually stir it into the egg mixture.

4 Put the custard into a bowl and stand it in the water to heat over a moderate heat.

5 Stir with a wooden spoon until all the sugar is dissolved and the mixture coats the back of the spoon.

6 Do not allow the custard to boil, or it will curdle.

7 Pour into a warmed serving jug and serve hot

8 If serving cold, place grease proof paper, cut to size, directly over sauce to prevent a skin forming.

Hot Cross Buns

Ingredients

25g (1 oz) fresh yeast or 1½ teaspoons dried yeast
1 teaspoon castor sugar
450g (1 lb.) flour
1 teaspoon salt
1 teaspoon mixed spice
½ teaspoon cinnamon
½ teaspoon nutmeg
100g (4 oz) butter
50g (2 oz) sugar
50g (2 oz) currants
50g (2 oz) raisins
25g (1 oz) candied peel
1 egg, beaten
300ml (½ pint) warm milk

For the glaze:
50g (2 oz) sugar
4½ tablespoons milk

Method

1 Cream the yeast with a teaspoon of sugar.

2 Mix the flour, salt and spices in a bowl.

3 Rub in the butter

4 Add the sugar, fruit and candied peel.

5 Pour in the beaten egg, warmed milk and yeast.

6 Beat the ingredients together and work to a soft dough.

7 Knead the dough on a floured board for 5-10 minutes.

8 Cover the dough with tinfoil and leave in a warm place for about an hour until the dough has doubled in size.

9 Divide into 12 pieces and shape into rounds.

10 Place the rounds on a greased baking sheet.

12 Cut crosses into each.

13 Cover and leave to rise in a warm place for a further 30 minutes.

14 Bake in a moderately hot oven for about 20 minutes or until golden brown.

15 Place in a cooling rack and glaze

For the glaze:

1 Dissolve the sugar with the warmed milk.

2 Brush the top of each bun with glaze whilst still warm.

3 Serve immediately, buttered and with jam or honey.

Oven: 200 °C

Carragheen Pudding

Ingredients

15g (½ oz) Carragheen Moss
900ml (1½ pints) milk
Grated rind of one lemon
50g (2 oz) sugar

Method

1 Wash the Carragheen and leave it to soak in cold water for 15 minutes. Drain well.

2 Put the Carragheen in a saucepan with the milk and the lemon rind.

3 Bring to the boil and simmer for about 15 minutes.

4 Add in the sugar and pour into a moistened mould.

5 Leave to set.

6 Turn out of the mould and decorate with whipped cream.

Bread and Butter Pudding

Ingredients

6 large slices of bread
40g (1½oz) butter or margarine
50g (2 oz) sugar
75g (3 oz) sultanas & sultanas
2 eggs
1 tablespoon honey
600ml (1 pint) milk
25g sugar for the top
A pinch of nutmeg

Method

1 Butter the bread on each side. If preferred: cut off the crusts.

2 Cut the bread into large pieces.

3 Cover the bottom of a greased 1ltr (2 pint) pie dish with a layer of bread, buttered side up.

4 Sprinkle with sugar and dried fruit.

5 Put another layer of bread, sugar and sultanas and final layer of bread on top, buttered side down.

6 Beat the eggs with the milk and honey.

7 Pour the egg mixture over the bread and leave to stand for at least ½ hour.

8 Sprinkle the top with sugar and nutmeg and bake in a moderately hot oven (180°C) for about 1 hour.

Brown Bread Ice Cream

Ingredients

45g (1½oz) wholemeal breadcrumbs
500ml whipping cream
180g (6½oz) demerara sugar
3 tablespoons of sweetish whiskey (e.g. Bushmills Malt, Midleton Special, or a good scotch)
drop of vanilla essence

Method

1 Spread the crumbs out on a large tray and toast under the grill, turning them regularly so they brown on all sides.

2 Remove from heat and leave to cool

3 Stir crumbs into cream with the remaining ingredients

4 Cover and chill for one hour

Restaurant Recipes

Lettercolm House

Lettercolm House is a Victorian manor house, one mile from the village of Timoleague, Co. Cork. As well as being a renowned restaurant it provides reasonably-priced accomodation. Resident chef, Karen Austin, conducts courses in vegetarian cookery. Queries should be addressed to Lettercolm House, Timoleague, Co. Cork. Tel: 023-46251

Carrot and Orange Soup

Ingredients

7 carrots approx.
1 large onion
1 large orange
100g (4 oz) red lentils
Vegetable stock
Salt and pepper

Method

1 Saute onion and chopped carrots.

2 Add vegetable stock, red lentils, grated zest of orange, salt and pepper.

3 Bring to boil and simmer 40 minutes approx.

4 Liquidise and add juice of orange.

5 Adjust seasoning.

6 Serve with a swirl of cream and chopped parsley.

Vegetable Mousakka

Ingredients

2 Large aubergines

Tomato Sauce:

3 cloves garlic
1 large onion
Olive oil
450g (1 lb.) tomatoes, skinned and deseeded or large tin tomatoes
2 tablespoons tomato puree
½ glass red wine
100g (4 oz) cooked brown lentils
Salt and pepper
2 tablespoons chopped fresh basil or 1 teaspoon dried basil

Savoury Custard:

200ml (5 fl oz) cream
3 egg yolks
150g (6 oz) cream cheese
50g (2 oz) parmesan
Salt and black pepper

Method

1 Slice aubergines, sprinkle with salt, leave for 20 mins approx., rinse and pat dry.

2 Sear the aubergines in olive oil on both sides.

3 Saute the onions until soft, add crushed garlic and cook for a further 2 minutes.

4 Stir in tomatoes, tomato puree, red wine, lentils, salt and pepper.

5 If using dried basil add now. Simmer away for 10 minutes. If using fresh basil add now.

6 Put cream, egg yolks and cream cheese in food processor and blend until smooth. Add parmesan cheese, salt and pepper.

7 Put a third of the tomato mixture in the bottom of an oven proof dish, cover with half of the aubergines then another third of the tomato mix with the remainder of the aubergines on top. Add the remainder of the tomato mix. Pour the savoury custard over the mixture and bake at 180°C for approx. 30 minutes until top is puffed and golden.

Summer Fruit Tart

Ingredients

1 Sweet pastry base - baked blind

Creme de patisserie:
3 egg yolks
60g (2 oz) sugar
20g (1 oz) flour
250ml (1/2 pint) milk
½ vanilla pod, split

Syrup:
100g (4 oz) sugar
100ml (¼ pint) water

For glaze:

2 tablespoons apricot jam
2 tablespoons water

Fresh fruit i.e. assortment of peaches, plums and berry fruits

Method

1 Beat egg yolks with half of the sugar, sift in flour and mix well.

2 Bring milk, the remaining sugar and vanilla pod to the boil.

3 Pour, in a slow stream, beating all the time onto the egg yolk mixture.

4 Return to saucepan and boil for 2 minutes.

5 Cool and pour into pastry base.

6 Dissolve sugar and water to make syrup.

7 Add peaches and plums to syrup and poach for 10 minutes. (Do not poach berry fruits)

8 Halve strawberries and arrange all of the fruit in a decorative pattern on top of the creme de patisserie.

9 Bring apricot jam and waster to the boil and strain.

10 Brush over fruit and serve.

Triskel Arts Centre Café

This café is situated pleasantly inside Cork's premier arts centre. It serves occasional meat dishes along with stunning vegetarian meals. The café features stained glass windows by internationally renowned artists Maud Cotter and James Scanlon (Scanlon's window is featured on the cover of this book). All queries to Triskel Arts Centre Café, Tobin Street, Cork. Tel: 021-272022

Tomato and Carrot Sauce

Ingredients

1 Large tin of tomatoes or 450g (1 lb.) fresh tomatoes, skinned
300ml (½ pint) water.
225g (½ lb.) carrots
2 tablespoons Soya sauce

Method

1 If using tinned tomatoes - liquidise. If using fresh tomatoes, place in a bowl of boiling water for a few minutes and use a fork or spoon to remove skins. Liquidise with the water.

2 Clean and grate carrots.

3 Place the liquidised tomatoes in a saucepan and add the grated carrot.

4 Simmer for 20 minutes until the carrot is tender.

5 When cooked add the Soya sauce and serve.

Stuffed Courgettes

Ingredients

4 large courgettes
100g (4 oz) brown rice
100g (4 oz) mushrooms
2 large tomatoes
2 tablespoons bean sprouts
1 onion
½ teaspoon cumin
½ teaspoon coriander
½ teaspoon garam marsala

Method

1 Cut each end of the courgettes and scoop out the pulp.

2 Chop the pulp into small pieces.

3 Cook the brown rice for 25 minutes.

4 Chop the mushrooms and tomatoes and bean sprouts finely.

5 Mix all the ingredients and stuff into the courgettes.

6 Place on an oiled tray and bake for 40 minutes at 190°C (375 F)

7 Serve with tomato sauce and a selection of fresh vegetables.

Chick Pea Soup

Ingredients

225g (½ lb.) chick peas - soaked overnight and cooked for ½-1hr approx.
100g (4 oz) brown rice, cooked
450g (1 lb.) parsnips chopped
450g (1 lb.) celery chopped
450g (1 lb.) onions chopped
2 teaspoons garam masala
2 teaspoons Soya sauce
1.2-2.4lt (2-4 pints) water or vegetable stock
2 tablespoons olive oil

Method

1 Heat the oil in a large saucepan.

2 Add the vegetables and saute for 10-15 minutes until softened.

3 Add the water or stock and cook for a further 10 minutes.

4 The garam masala and Soya sauce can be added to the mixture at this stage and cook for a further 15 minutes.

5 Half the soup can be liquidised and added back to the saucepan - this thickens the soup.

6 Serve in bowls and garnish with yoghurt, parsley or croutons.

Garlic and Pine Kernal Tartlets

Ingredients

Pastry:
225g (8 oz) plain flour
½ teaspoon salt
100g (4 oz) butter or margarine
2-3 tablespoons cold water

225g (8 oz) pastry
150g (5 oz) butter
6 cloves garlic crushed
4 tablespoons grated parmesan cheese
1 tablespoon fresh chopped basil
4 tablespoon pine kernel (chopped roughly)
Freshly ground black pepper
Beaten egg

Method

1 Roll out the pastry and line four individual fluted flan tins.

2 Place in the fridge for minutes

3 Place the butter, garlic, cheese and the chopped basil in a processor and blend until smooth.

4 Mix in the pine nuts and add pepper to taste.

5 Line the pastry cases with foil or grease proof paper and bake blind in the oven for 10 mins at 190°C (375 F).

6 Divide the mixture between the four cases and glaze with beaten egg.
7 Bake for 20-25 minutes until pastry is golden brown.

Baked Lemon Cheesecake

Ingredients

900g (2 lbs) low fat cheese
175g (6 oz) castor sugar
3 large eggs
Juice of 1 lemon
350g (12 oz) digestive biscuits
150g (5 oz) butter
25cm (10 inch) round quiche tin

Method

1 Place the biscuits in a food processor and blend until the biscuits are crumbled.

2 Melt butter and add biscuit crumb to it.

3 Place mixture in tin and flatten out with metal spoon.

4 Beat the cheese, sugar, eggs and juice until smooth, or alternatively place all these ingredients in the processor at full power for 2 minutes.

5 Pour this mixture into the prepared tin and bake at 190°C (375 F) for 40minutes - 1hr approx. in the centre of the oven.

6 Cover with foil if it is becoming too brown.

7 It should be firm to the touch, with a slight spring, when cooked.

8 Allow to cool and serve with cream.

The Quay Co-op

The Quay Co-op restaurant was established over ten years ago and is well established in all of the guide books. The building also includes a wholefood shop from which many of the more unusual ingredients found in this book can be bought. All queries to The Quay Co-op, Sullivan's Quay, Cork City. Tel: 021-317660

Vegetable Tempura with Dipping Sauce

Ingredients

1 Aubergine sliced into 1cm (½ inch) thickness
2 Courgettes cut into 1cm (½ inch) thickness
4 Carrots sliced quite thinly
1 Pepper (red or yellow) sliced
1 Cauliflower broken into florets
1 Broccoli stalk broken into florets
4 Whole radish
100g (4 oz) mange-tout
100g (4 oz) mushrooms
4 Spring onions chopped into 5cm (2 inch) pieces

Batter:

100g (4 oz) sieved white flour
A pinch of salt
1 beaten egg yolk
175ml (6 fl oz) water

Dip:

50g (2 oz) light tahini
6 tablespoons hot water
3½ tablespoons Soya sauce
½ tablespoon honey
½ tablespoon fine-grated ginger

Method

1 Make batter by combining all batter ingredients without overmixing and chill until needed. (Do not worry about lumps).

2 Whisk tahini and hot water smooth, then beat in remaining ingredients.

3 Heat oil to 180° C (350 F) in Deep Fat Fryer.

4 Coat vegetables in batter, shake off excess and drop in oil, frying only one layer at a time.

5 Keep cooked pieces warm while frying remainder.

6 Serve on warmed plates with sauce in bowl, sprinkle with sesame seeds. Garnish with julienne ginger, slices of peppers, coconut strips and eat with chopsticks.

Aubergine and Tomato Red Wine Fyllo with Cucumber Raita and Goats Cheese and Walnut Salad

Aubergine and Tomato Red Wine Fyllo

Ingredients

300g (11 oz) Aubergine
7 Cardamom Pod Seeds
¼ teaspoon Allspice (ground)
¼ teaspoon Cayenne pepper

1 Whole bayleaf
¾ teaspoon sugar
110ml Red Wine
110ml Water
2 teaspoon tomato puree
90ml Shoyu
Olive oil
2 minced cloves of garlic
100g (4 oz) fine breadcrumbs
1 small, finely chopped onion
Pinch salt
50g (2 oz) finely chopped parsley
225g (8 oz) fresh, chopped tomatoes
16 sheets of Fyllo pastry 22.5cm x 15cm (9" x 6")

Method

1 Saute aubergines in olive oil until tender.

2 Add cardamom seeds, allspice, cayenne pepper, bayleaf, sugar, red wine, water, tomato puree and shoyu and simmer until reduced by a third (Do not let aubergines get mushy).

3 Cool sauce and mix in the minced garlic cloves, breadcrumbs, finely chopped onion, salt, chopped parsley and chopped tomatoes.

4 Lightly butter 8 sheets of fyllo pastry on both sides.

5 Place remaining 8 sheets on top and butter again.

6 Put a large dessertspoon of filling at the top of each sheet, fold in2.5cm (1 inch) on either side and roll up.

7 Continue with remainder and place on a tray covered in grease

proof paper and place in a pre-heated oven 240°C (460 F) for 15 to 20 minutes until golden brown.

Raita

Ingredients

½ Cucumber, peeled and diced
250ml (½ pint) natural, unsweetened yoghurt
1 minced clove of garlic
1 teaspoon chopped fresh mint
Pinch of salt

Method

1 Combine all ingredients.

2 Chill until needed. Use within 24 hours.

Goats Cheese and Walnut Salad

Ingredients

Walnut Vinaigrette:

1 teaspoon salt
2 teaspoons red wine vinegar
3 tablespoons olive oil
4 tablespoons walnut oil
Freshly ground black pepper

Salad:
1 head of oakleaf lettuce

1 soft goats cheese
4 tablespoons of chopped walnut

Method

1 Combine all vinaigrette ingredients and leave to stand until required.

2 Wash lettuce, and divide between four serving bowls.

3 Slice the goats cheese into four and lay on top of lettuce.

4 Sprinkle each dish with a tablespoon of chopped walnuts.

5 Finally drizzle vinaigrette over each salad.

Serve the aubergine, red wine and tomato fyllos hot or cold with a ramekin of raita and a bowl of the walnut salad.

Cantaloupe and Ginger Sorbet with Blackberry Coulis

Ingredients

Sorbet:
1 Ripe cantaloupe melon, peeled, seeded and pureed
225g (8 oz) granulated sugar
110ml (3 fl oz) water
2 tablespoons lemon juice
100ml (3¼ fl oz) ginger ale.

Coulis:
250g (9 oz) fresh blackberries
4 teaspoons water
4 teaspoons caster sugar

Method

1 Heat 225g (8 oz) sugar and 110ml (3½ fl oz) water gently until sugar dissolves.

2 Boil hard for about 20 minutes until syrupy (sugar thread stage)

3 Add lemon juice and ginger ale and cool.

4 Add melon pulp and pour into a polythene container and freeze overnight.

5 Turn into a bowl and beat until smooth and creamy. Return to freezer until firm.

6 Blend blackberries, sugar and water.

7 Put the ingredients through a sieve.

8 Slowly bring to the boil.

9 Boil for 1 minute to a clear glossy sauce.

10 Cool and chill.

11 Serve by shaping sorbet with 2 large spoons. Place coulis on plates and place sorbet on top and garnish with fresh mint leaves.

Blazing Salads

Blazing Salads is located in the prestigious Powerscourt Townhouse Centre. All of their recipes are dairy, wheat and sugar free - so making them ideal for vegans and other people with special diets. These recipes were prepared by Lorraine Fitzmaurice. All queries to Blazing Salads, Powerscourt Townhouse Centre, Clarendon Street, Dublin 2. Tel: 01-6719552

Carrot and Cashew Nut Soup

Ingredients

1 Medium onion diced finely
75g (3 oz) cashew nut pieces
675g (1½ lb.) carrots cut into large rounds
3 medium potatoes diced (optional)
900ml (1½ pints) water
Sunflower oil
Salt and pepper
Chopped fresh parsley

Method

1 In a large saucepan saute onion, cashew nuts in a little sunflower oil until golden brown.

2 Add carrots, potatoes (if using) and saute for a further 5 minutes.

3 Season with salt and pepper.

4 Add the water, cover and bring to boil.

5 Simmer for 20 minutes.

6 Liquidise well and season further.

7 Garnish with chopped fresh parsley.

Steamed Vegetables in Sweet and Sour Sauce

Ingredients

1 Carrot cut thickly
¼ turnip diced
1 small parsnip cut thickly
½ cauliflower broken into florets
1 small broccoli stalk broken into florets
1 courgette cut thickly
25g (1 oz) mange tout
1 packet fresh baby sweet corn

Method

1 In a large saucepan put ½cm (¼ inch) water and a pinch of salt.

2 Add carrots and turnip, cover with a tight lid, bring to the boil, then reduce to the lowest heat possible and allow to steam.

3 After approx. 5 minutes add parsnip, cauliflower, broccoli and cover for a further ten minutes.

4 Add the courgette, mangetout and corn, cover and steam until all the vegetables are tender.

(Editor's note) If your lid is not tight-fitting enough, you will probably need to add extra water during the cooking process.

Sweet and Sour Sauce

Ingredients

2 tsp Arrowroot or cornflower
1.5 fl. oz water
1.5 fl. oz shoyu
Juice of half a lemon
7 ml Apple juice concentrate
pinch of ginger
coriander or parsley to garnish

Method

1 Blend all ingredients together.

2 Heat until sauce has thickened, stirring well to avoid lumps.

3 Pour over tossed, steamed vegetables.

Apple and Pear Crumble

Ingredients

2 dessert apples peeled and sliced
2 dessert pears peeled and sliced
25 g (1 oz) raisins
50g (2 oz) fine oatflakes
50g (2 oz) jumbo oatflakes
25g (1oz) mix of pumpkin, sunflower and sesame seed.
3 tablespoons of apple concentrate
3 tablespoons of sunflower oil

Method

1 Steam the apples and pears in a little water until tender, this takes approx. 5 minutes

2 Place fruit and liquid from same in oven proof dish together with 2 tablespoons of apple concentrate and raisins

3 In a bowl blend the oats and seeds with the sunflower oil and remaining apple concentrate

4 Spoon oat mixture over fruit and place in preheated oven (190°C) for 20-30 mins until golden brown

Cafe Paradiso

The Cafe Paradiso is a new specialist vegetarian restaurant just opened up by Dennis Cotter (no relation of the Editor's) who was chef at the Quay Co-op for five years. It is situated opposite Jury's Hotel in Cork. All queries to Cafe Paradiso, 16 Lancaster Quay, Western Road, Cork City. Tel: 021-277939

Broccoli Mousse With Warm Tomato Vinaigrette

The Mouse

Ingredients

2 tablespoons olive oil or butter
450g (10 oz) Broccoli florets
300ml light vegetable stock
3 large eggs
4-5 tablespoons cream
Salt & pepper

Method

1 Preheat oven to 180°C. Half-fill a roasting tray with hot water and place on middle shelf

2 Saute broccoli in oil for 3 minutes

3 Add stock, bring to boil, cover and simmer for 5 minutes

4 Cook 5 minutes more uncovered

5 Remove from heat, pureé in a blender and season

6 Add eggs and cream and blend in

7 Butter six ramekins and fill each one with mixture. Place ramekins in the roasting tray and bake for 35 minutes

8 Allow to stand 5-10 minutes before turning out

The Vinaigrette

Ingredients

3-4 tomatoes, skinned and chopped
4-5 tablespoons red wine vinegar
150ml olive oil
30g shallots finely chopped (or a two-inch piece of the white of a leek)
Small bunch chives, finely chopped
Salt & pepper

Method

1 Mix everything thoroughly and warm gently in a pan

Cheese Gougeres with Safron-buttered Root Vegetables on Creamed Leeks

THE PASTRY

Ingredients

290 ml hot water
100g (4 oz) butter
170g (7 oz) flour
100g (4 oz) cheese (Swiss-style or cheddar)

3 medium-sized eggs
pinch of cayenne
½ tsp. salt

Method

1 Preheat oven to (220°c)

2 Place water and butter in a saucepan and bring to boil

3 Add flour and beat over low heat until smooth and shiny.

4 Add an egg and beat again until smooth.

5 Repeat process with remaining eggs before adding cheese and seasoning

6 Now either pipe dough around a large flan tin or pizza tray; or make 4 individual rings on a greased tray. Bake in oven for 10 minutes, then turn down heat to 100°C and bake for 5-10 minutes more.

The Vegetables

Ingredients

A selection of fresh root vegetables (e.g. Carrots, white turnip, swede, parsnip, celeraic)

Method

1 Dice the vegetables

2 Steam them until they are just tender

3 Season with salt and pepper

The Butter

Ingredients

200 g butter
a few sprigs of parsley
rind of ¼ lemon.
pinch of cayenne pepper
¼ tsp. (or more!) saffron threads in 2 tablespoons of hot water

Method

Blend everything

The Leeks

Ingredients

2 leeks
2 cloves garlic
50 g (2 oz) butter
250 ml cream
pinch of nutmeg
salt & pepper

Method

1 chop leeks and stew with garlic in the butter for approx. 10 minutes

2 add cream and seasoning

3 simmer until cream reduces by one third

4 blend half and replace in pot.

The Finale

If your timing is brilliant, place warm leeks on a warm plate, place a straight-from-the-oven gougere ring on top; then toss the hot vegetables in the saffron butter and pour into the centres of the gougeres. If not, everything reheats well. Serve with rice or potatoes for the root addicts.

Sauteed Pears with Ginger and Walnuts

Ingredients

4 pears peeled and cut in quarters or sixths
50 g (2 oz) walnut halves
8 thin slices of fresh ginger
½ glass of white wine
½ glass of ginger syrup, homemade or deli-bought

Method

1 Gently saute pears in butter with walnuts for about six minutes, turning once.

2 Add fresh ginger, cook for two minutes more

3 Add wine and syrup and allow to bubble once

4 serve immediately with something, cold, creamy and rich (ice cream!)

Mainistir House Hostel

Mainistir House Hostel located on the Aran Islands must be the last Vegetarian eatinghouse before America. Cook Joël d'Anjou refuses to allow his establishment to be labelled a restaurant as most of the food is presented as a buffet, so it doesn't follow the usual divisions of starter, maincourse and dessert. Whatever way its presented its fame has spread far and wide. Below are some samples from Joël's buffet. All queries to Mainistir House Hostel, Inis Mór, Galway. Tel: 099-61169

Tomato Preserve

Ingredients

900g (2 lbs) tomatoes
900g (2 lbs) sugar
300ml (½ pint) water
1 Vanilla bean pod

Method

1 Place tomatoes in boiling water and leave to stand for 5-10 minutes.

2 Skin and cut into small pieces, saving seeds and juices.

3 Over a moderate heat disolve sugar and water.

4 Add tomatoes and leave to stand for 35 minutes.

5 Add vanilla pod and leave for another 10 minutes.

6 Allow to cool and serve with yoghurt, fromage frais or ricotta cheese.

Carmelised Onions And Prunes

Ingredients

3.6Kg (4 lbs) onions
900g (1 lb) dried prunes
900ml (1 pint) water
225g (8 oz) butter
Salt and pepper to taste

Method

1 Peel onions and cut into circles.

2 Place in a heavy saucepan with water and prunes.

3 Bring to a vigorous boil and let simmer until water has almost evaporated.

4 Add butter and let it cook slowly until it is golden brown and all the ingredients are reduced to ¼ of its original contents.

5 This may be served with nutty dishes or a sweet and sour accompinament with tofu.

Cook Up Rice

Ingredients

2 cups basmati rice
1 dessert spoon butter
1 cup of blackeye beans
1.2 lt (2 pints) coconut milk
Tabasco sauce or few chopped chillies

2 onions
Salt and pepper to taste

Method

1 Soak beans overnight, cook and leave to stand.

Coconut Milk:

1 Grate 1 coconut and add to water.

2 Let stand, squeeze and discard shredded coconut.

3 Fry onions in butter until transparent.

4 Add rice and strained beans, then add milk and allow to cook for 12 minutes until all the milk has been absorbed.

5 Add tobasco sauce and a knob of butter and serve.

Bibliography

Irish Cook Books

The Ballymaloe Cookbook by Myrtle Allen, publishede by Gill & MacMillan
A Feast Of Irish Cooking by Molly O'Neill, Dolmen Press
The Irish Gourmet by Connie O'Mahony, Thorsons
Traditional Irish Recipes by George L Thompson, The O'Brien Press
The Irish Heritage Cookbook by McLoughlin and McSpiritt, Careers and Educational Publishers
Irish Country Kitchen by Anon, Mac Publications
Irish Farmhouse Recipes by Anon, Mac Publications
Irish Traditional Food by Theodora Fitzgibbon, Gill & MacMillan
Land Of Milk And Honey, The Story Of Irish Traditional Food & Drink by Bríd Mahon, Poolbeg Press
Irish Country Recipes by Ann and Sarah Gomar, Ravette Books Ltd.

Vegetarian Cook books

The Supreme Vegetarian Cookbook by Rose Elliot, Fontana
Simply Delicious Vegetables by Darina Allen, Gill & MacMillan, Spring 1994
The Bridgestone Vegetarian Guide To Ireland, Bridgestone Press - not a recipe book but an indispensible guide to restaurants and wholefood suppliers

Appendix

Oven Temperatures

Degrees Centigrade	*Degrees Fahrenheit*	*Regulo (for gas cookers)*
115-35	240-80	¼-½
135-60	280-320	1
160-70	320-40	3
170-85	340-70	4
185-205	370-400	5-6
205-25	400-40	7
225-50	440-80	8-9

Index

E

F

G

R

S

T

V

W

Notes

Notes

Notes

Notes

Notes

Notes